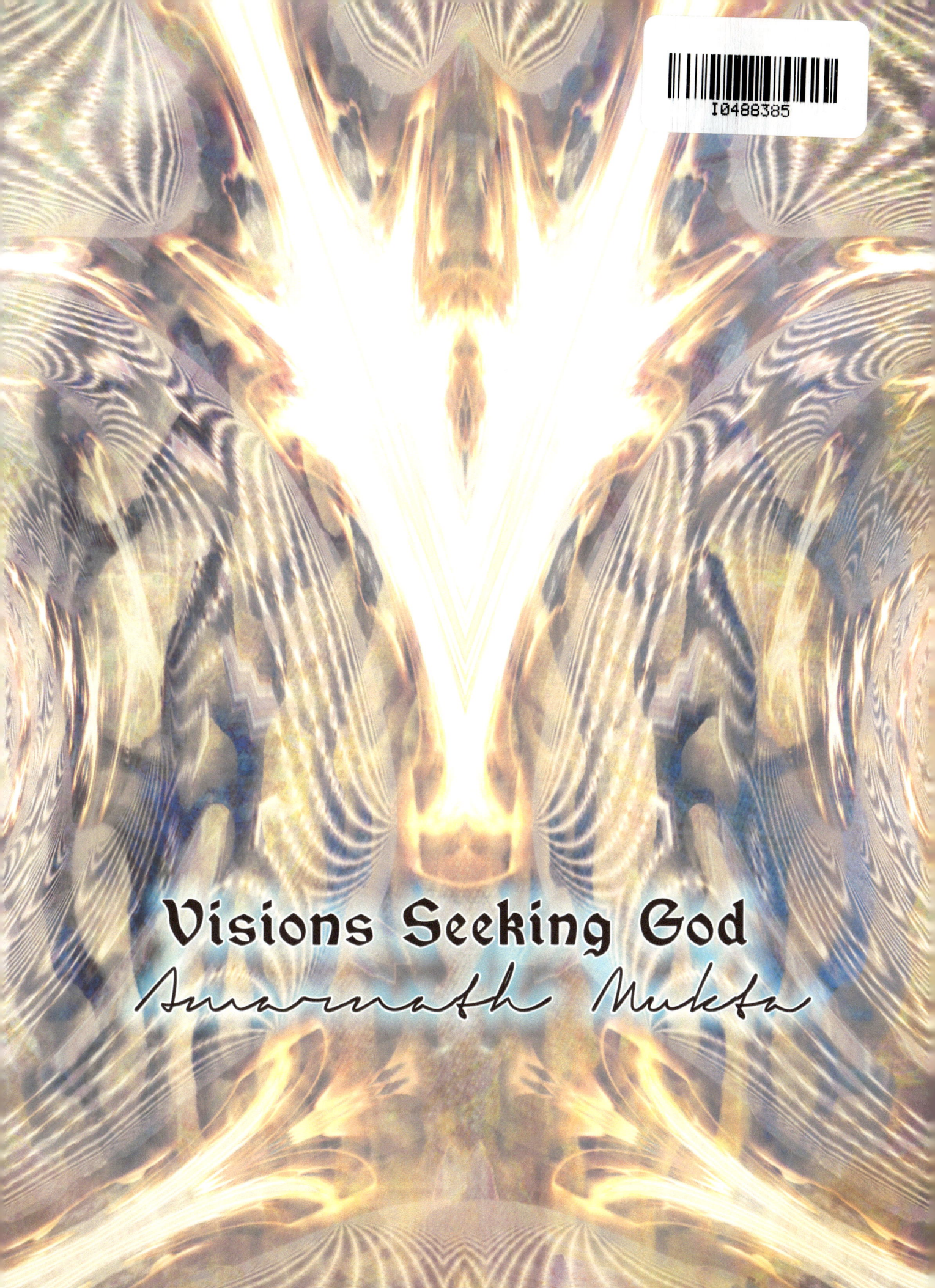

Visions Seeking God

Amarnath Mukta

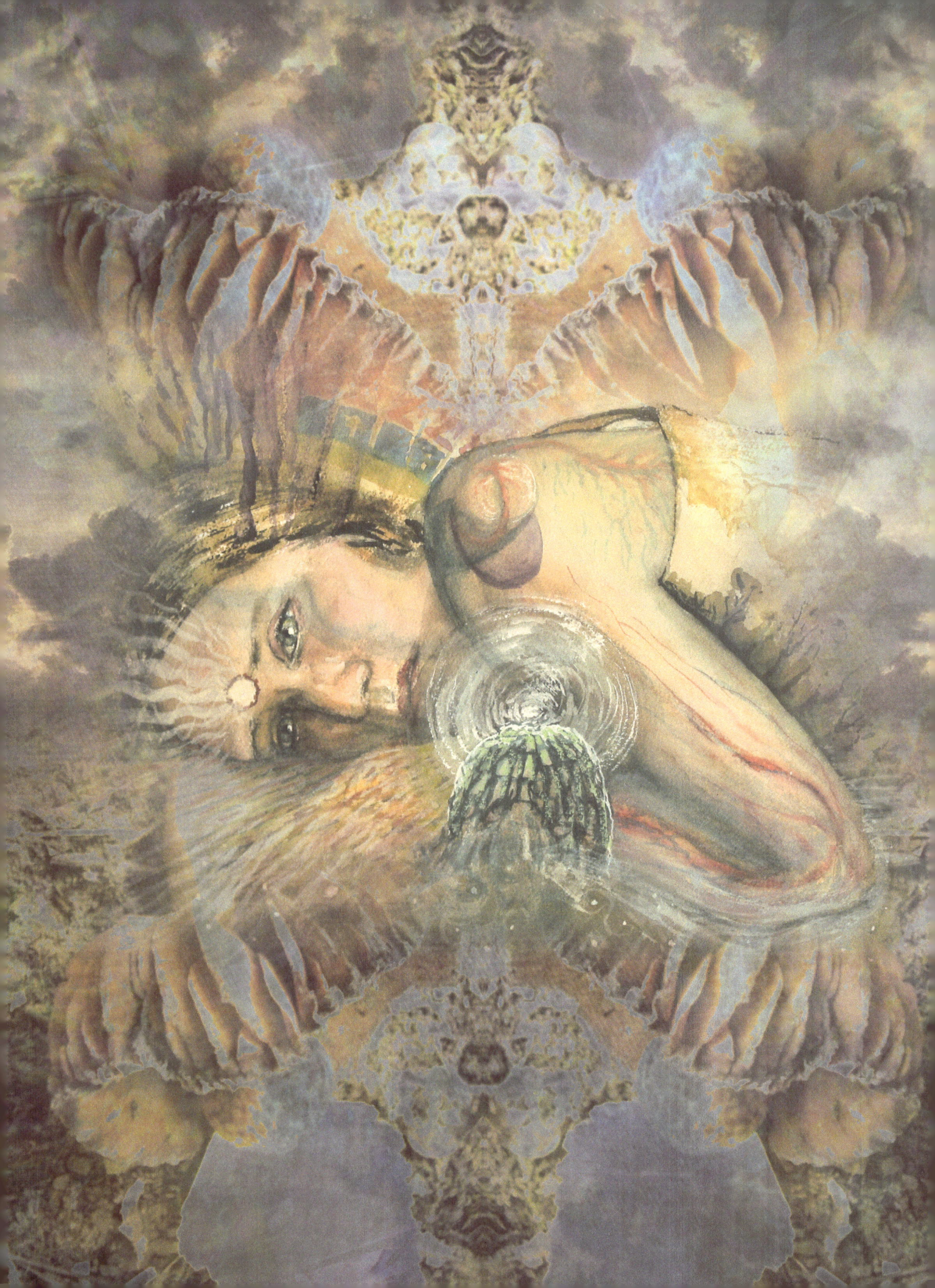

Namaskar
The absolute reality residing within my Being bows, as if in a mirror,
to the absolute reality residing within your Being.

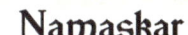

In order to receive the visions in their fullest form, browse slowly, entering each piece
with an innocence of eye. Unravel the pattern your mind is accustomed to and feel a
deeper silence, as your brain is humbled to your heart. Your heart is the seat of God.
Silence and God are one. Silence your heart's many waves and feel the true depth of
unity within your soul's vessel. As many of these images are over seven feet to the
longer, and have taken years to paint, they take time to understand. As you sit with an
image, things will begin to happen. You will notice new things emerging, and initial
impressions being swallowed by them. Let this dance happen; It is not until a movie
is finished that the film can be wholly contemplated.

Aum Namah Shivaya
(I bow to the absolute consciousness)

May divinity enter your heart in an unbroken stream
and overflow out to the world around you
transforming woe to wonder in weary eyes.

"Akashic Mandalandscape"

The left side of the mural is where the eye naturally begins reading. It represents the birth of creation. The stars have just spread across the cosmos. Our blue planet, Terra, is formed of a celestial sea, rolling in on a great wave, as northern lights dance above the earth. Moving to the right, we enter the wheel of space/time continuum. The phases of the moon indicate its revolving nature. The next ring of orbital mandalas and tunnels depict matter coming into and out of existence, guided by the underlying pattern of life stored in the Akashic records. The mandalas within are of twelve-fold nature, like the precession of the equinoxes in the zodiac, hours on a clock's face, or the twelve disciples around Jesus Christ. The wheel of time is also the wheel of life. The spokes all point to the same absolute truth of God in the center. Moving to the right half of the Mandala, the arms are forming into our neurons and DNA. This represents the light of God penetrating into the most refined level of our physiology. We move from Galactic scale (outward awareness) to Nano scale (inward awareness). The landscape of mountains and fields of flowers bring the viewer back to his or her own scale. In surrendering to God on both planetary and atomic scales of Being, we attain liberation. The stream of doves flying toward the sun represent the pure angelic souls ascending to heaven. The sun is the ever-giving sustainer of life, our Lord. Upon contact with the sun (the Son), the doves become their full effulgent angelic form. The total depiction is of one journey, or cycle: from absolute into manifestation and back to absolute again. This painting sheds light on the age old questions: Where do I come from? Who am I? To where am I going?

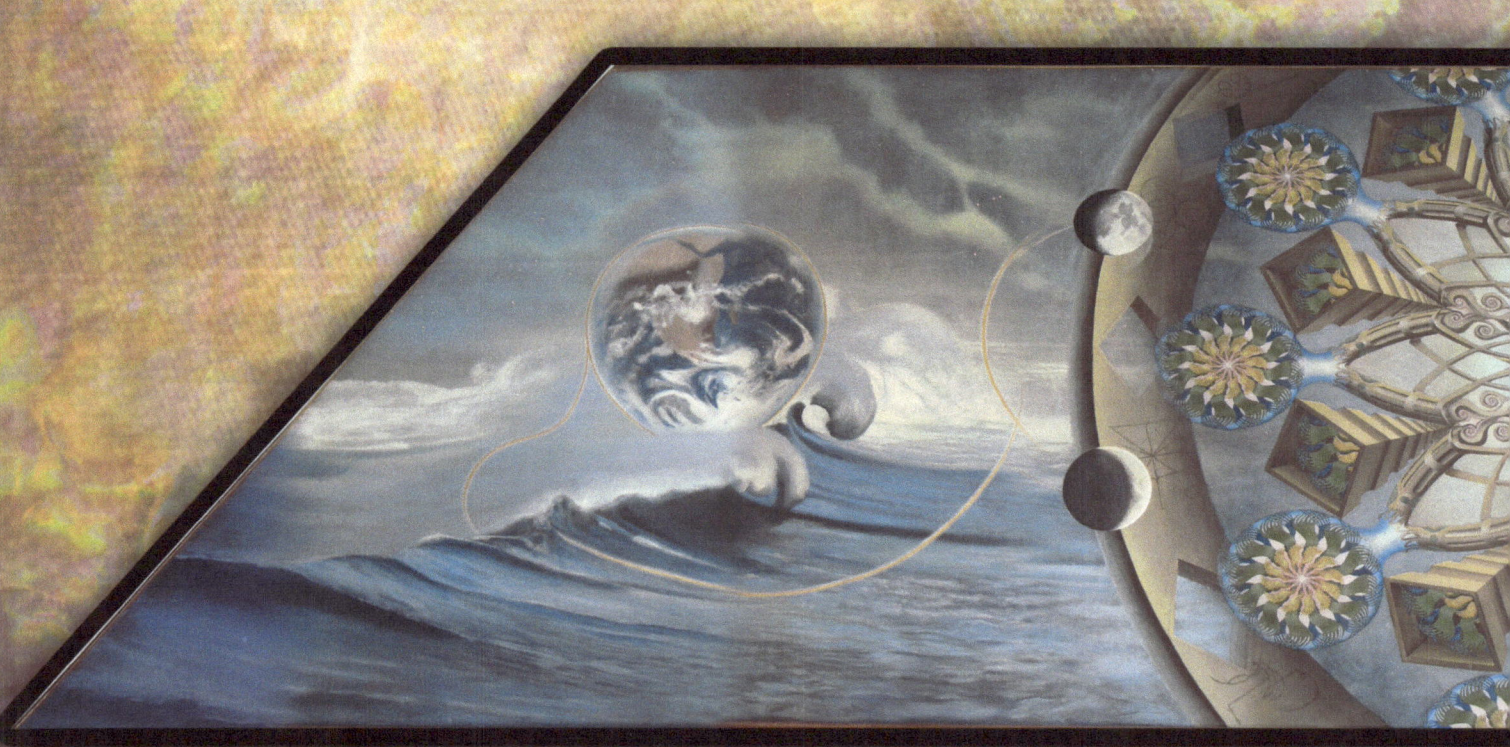

Acrylic and opelescent topaz on inclined wall panel.

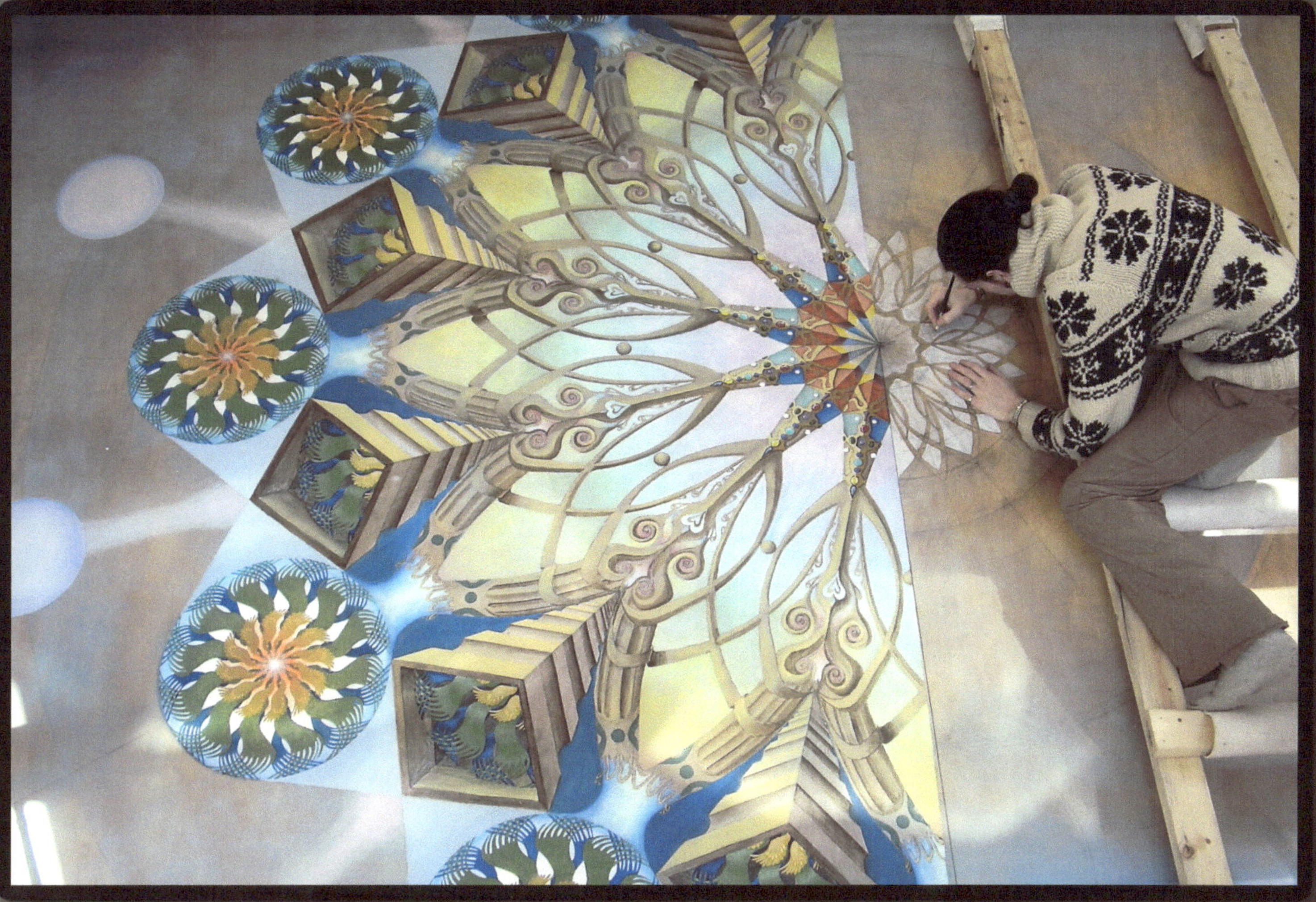

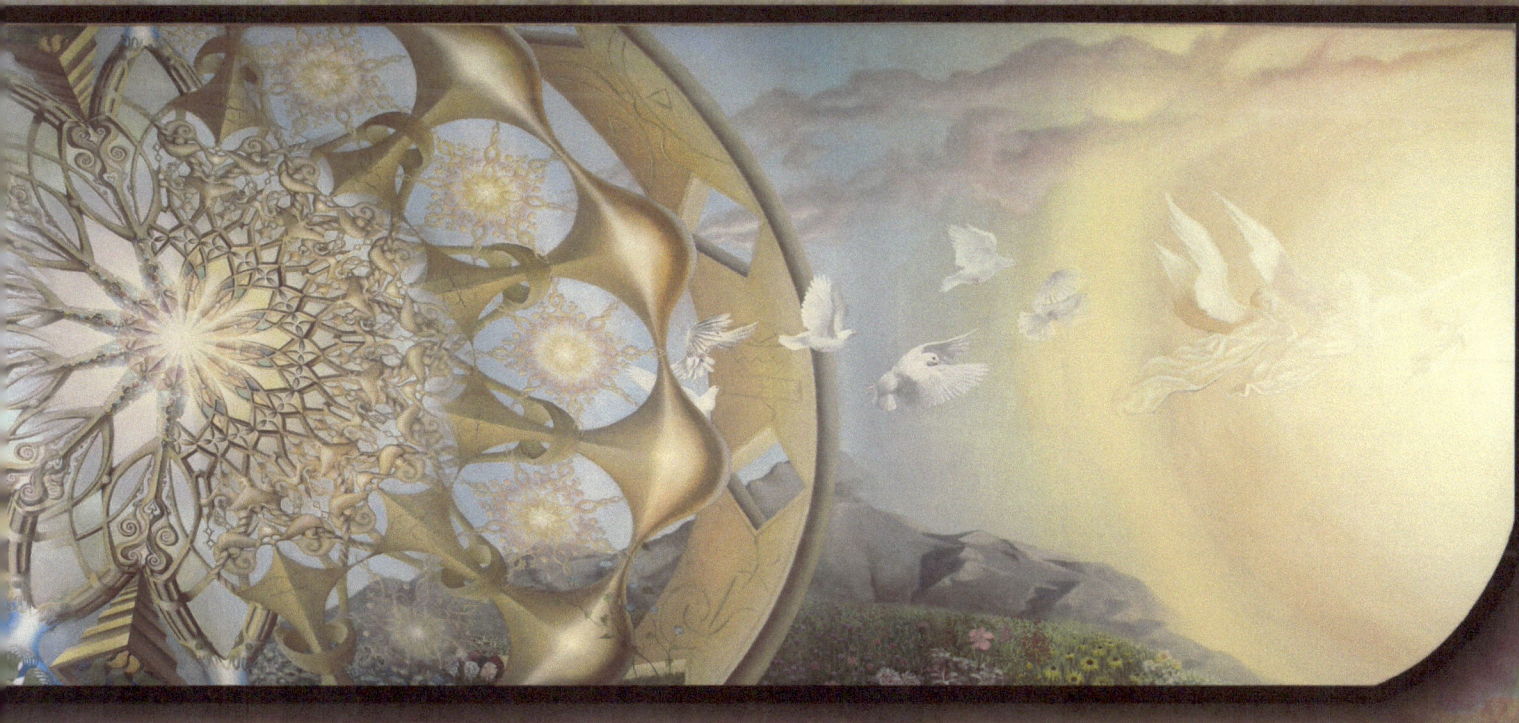

Photograph of me working on the center during an early stage of the mural's growth.

8' X 33'.   2007 to 2010.

"Twenty Twelve Nataraja"

Is a devotional painting for Lord Shiva. He is depicted lying in the ocean of Amrita. The three white lines on his forehead (representing the three worlds) become the sails of the vessal to cross the ocean of transmigration. From his navel, the power of creation emminates, spilling down below the surface of manifestation to it's source, the pure consciosness of the Shiva Lingam. Painted within the blue orb is Nataraja performing his eternal dance, coverered beneath crackled layers. In the root, Kali dances as Mary turns from the cross to face eternal reality. The center focal point has a ruby cabochon as a sun-like bindu for the celestial story to unfold around. The Sanskrit circumambulating the painting's border says "Aum Namah Shivaya" {I bow to the absolute consciousness}

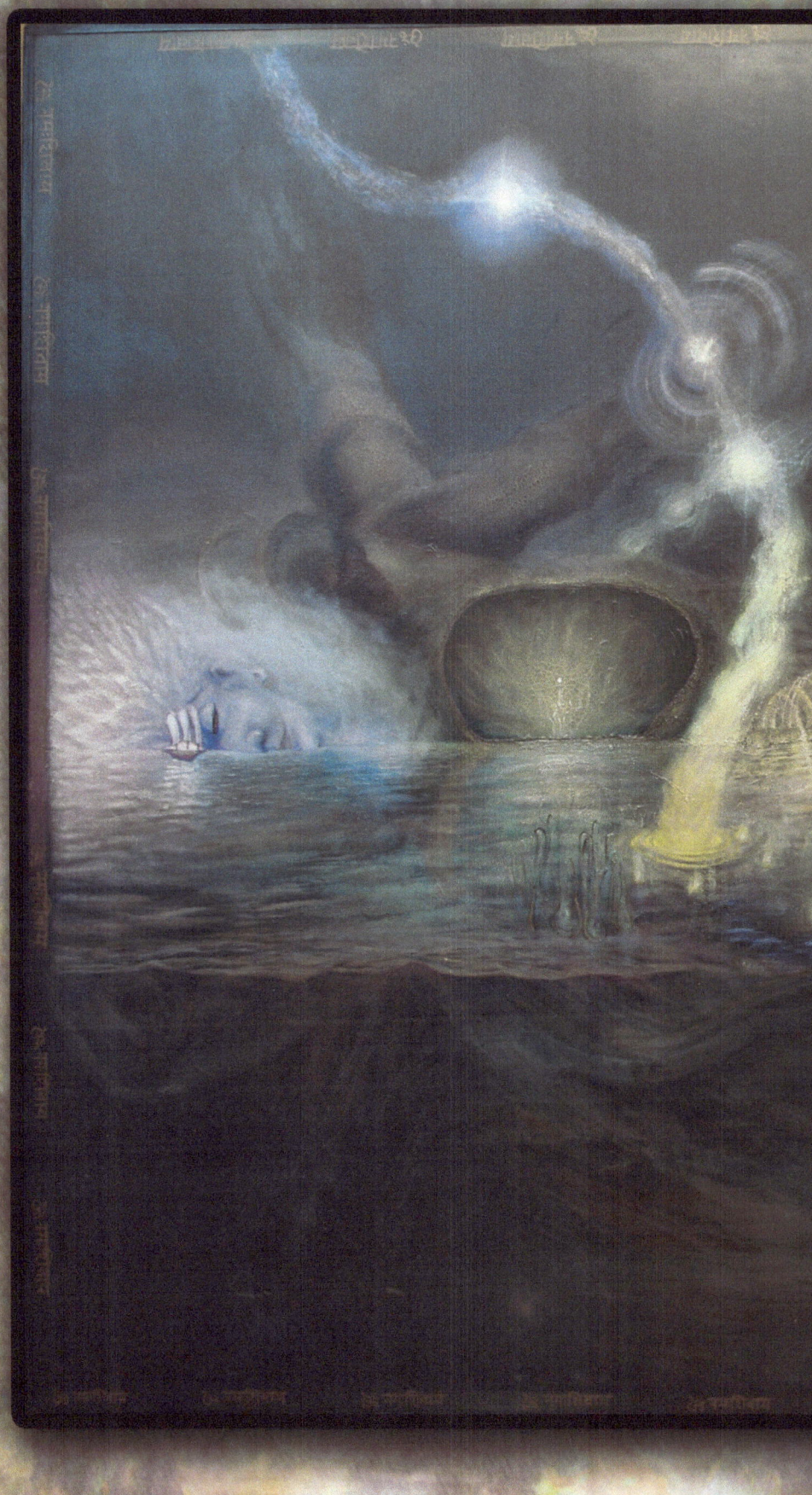

58" X 88"   2004 - 2010

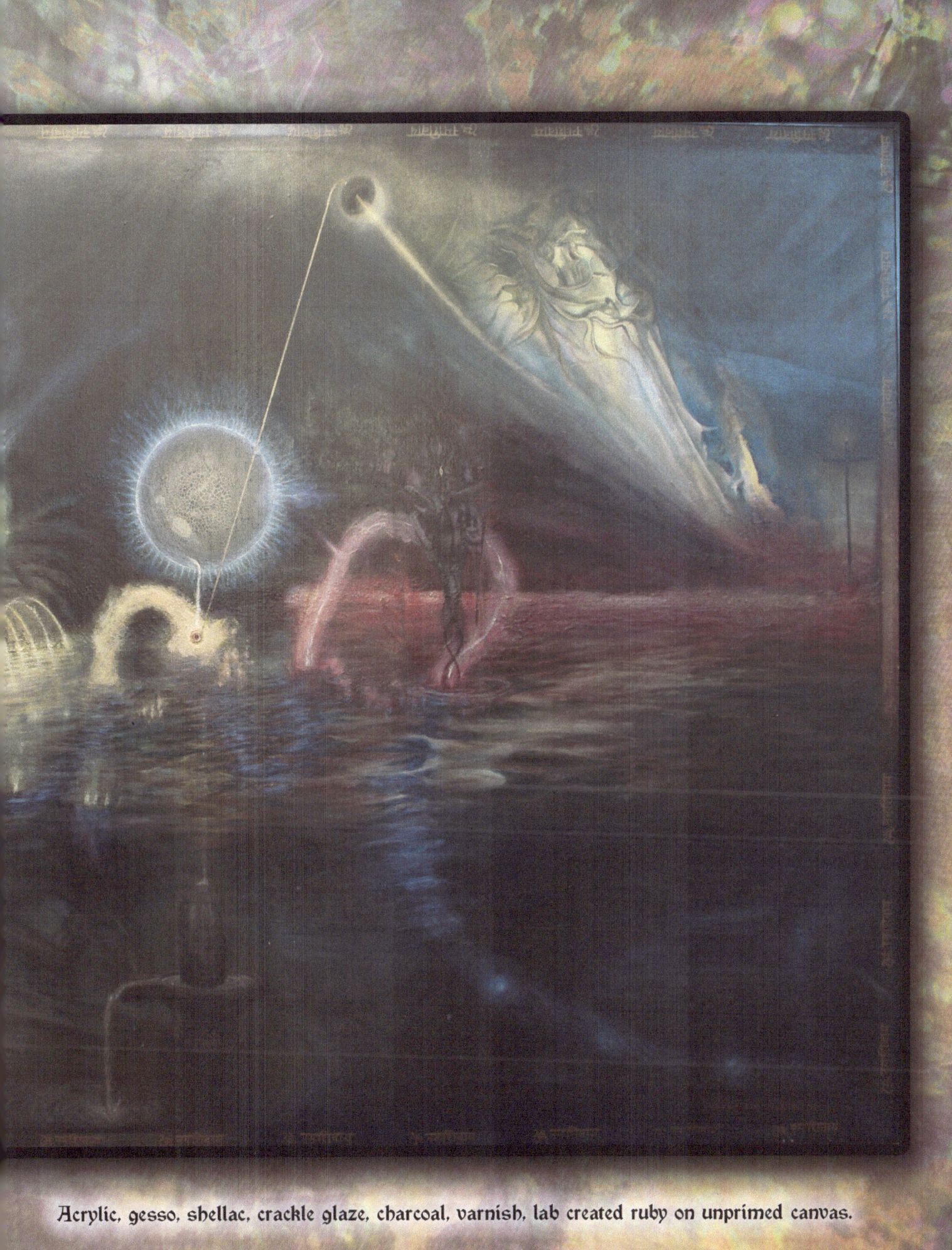

Acrylic, gesso, shellac, crackle glaze, charcoal, varnish, lab created ruby on unprimed canvas.

"I Are; We Am"

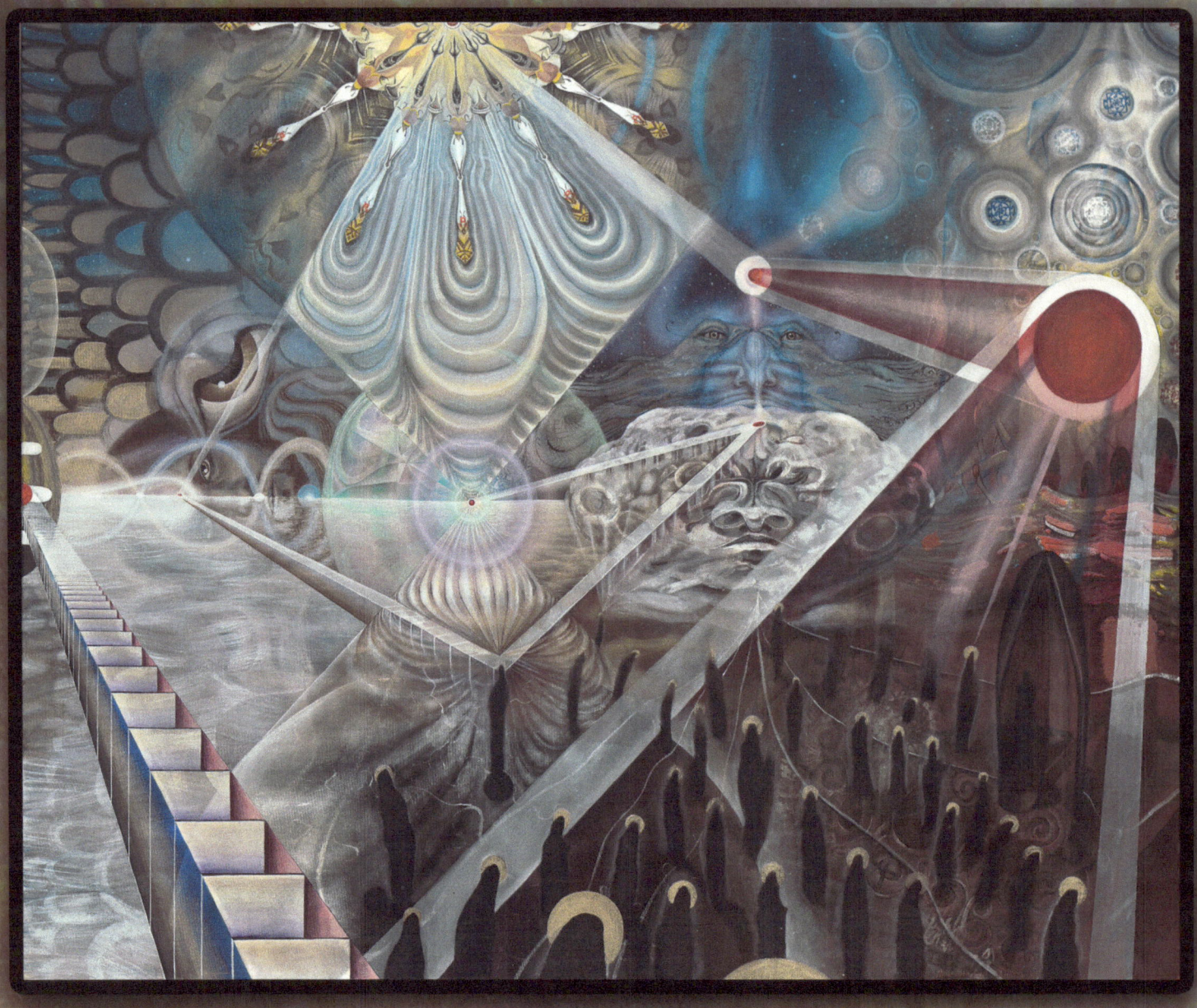

Acrylic on unprimed canvas.   48" X 60"   2006 - 2008

"I Are" is the most condensed way to express a personal identification with the universe; "We Am" is the most condensed way to express our collective unity. An alternate title is "As the Universe is Serpentine in Motion, it is Pyramidal in Structure." This painting is about the soul's journey through a seemingly paradoxical universe, ultimately finding the paradox to be the very dimensional structure of manifestation.

{right page:} The left side of Dharma of the Sleeper Yo-Yo depicts the earth as a Yo-Yo in God's hand, suspended for a moment before climbing the thread of dimensions back to the creator. The center column is the ascension of our consciousness and DNA. On the right is the journey of the individual soul through an infinite flatland back to source, a Shiva Lingam at the vanishing point.

"Dharma of the Sleeper Yo-Yo"

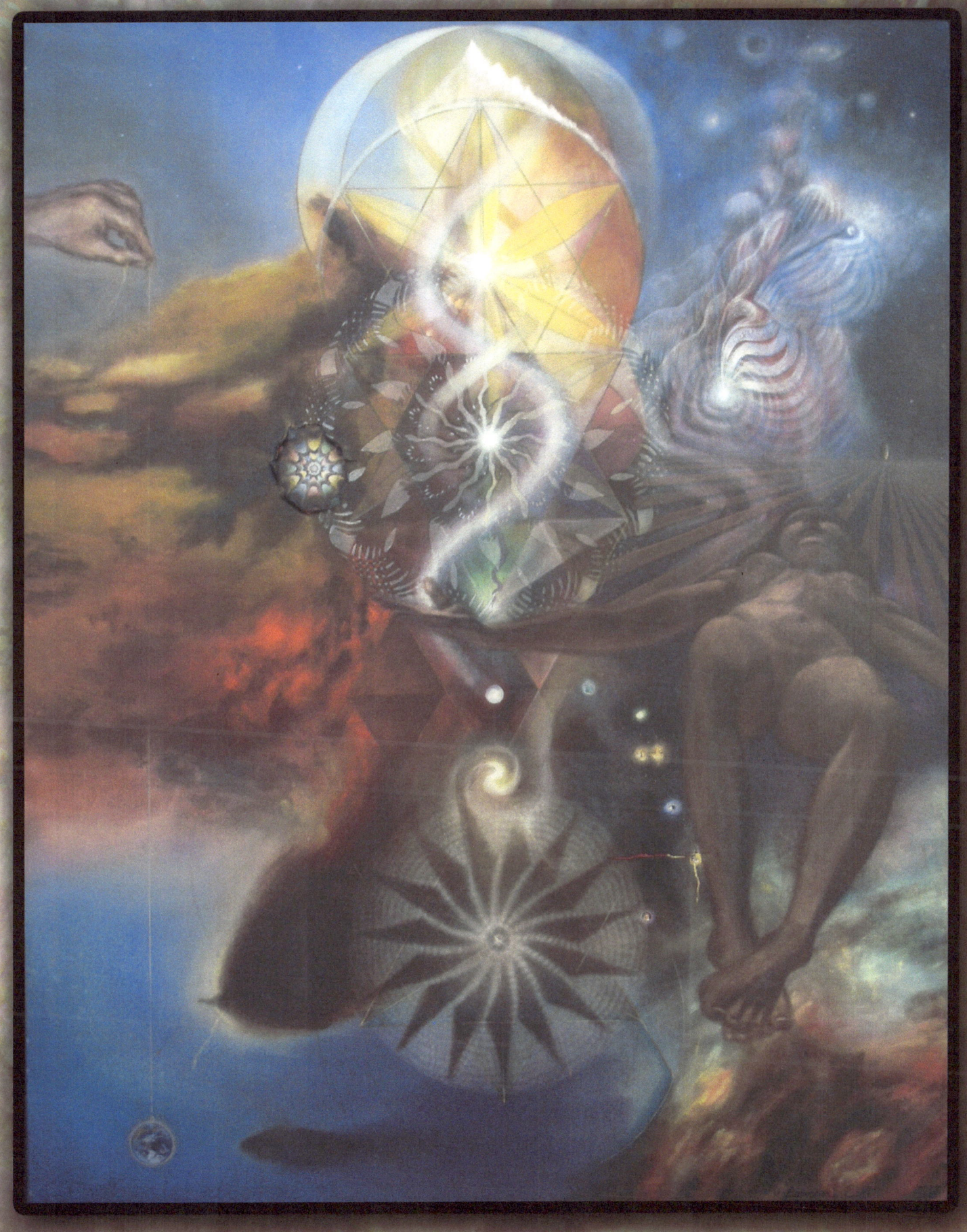

Acrylic on unprimed Canvas.   60" X 48"   2007 - 2010

"Procession of the Three Worlds"

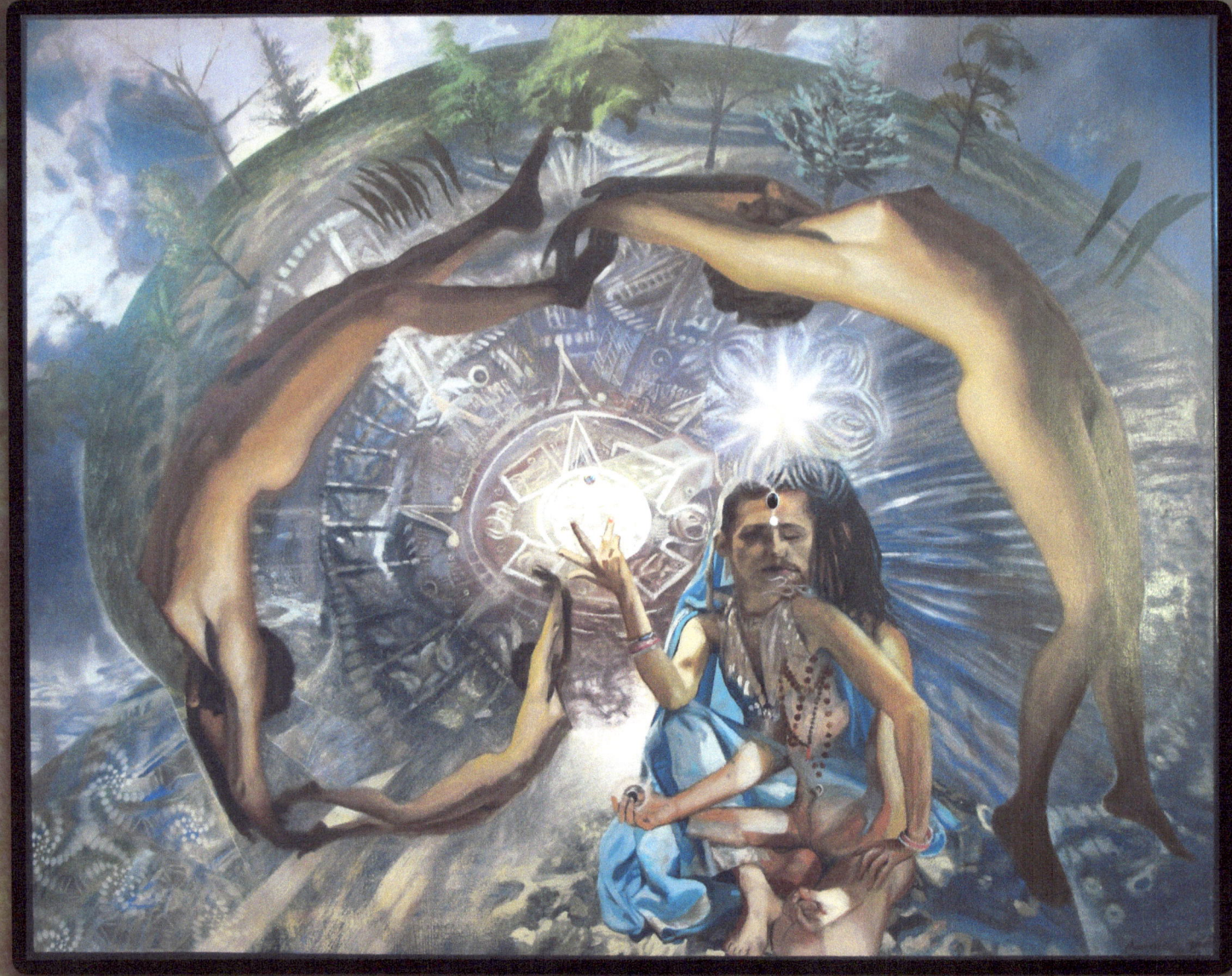

Oil and acrylic on cradled panel with inlaid natural stones: opalescent topaz (titanium dioxide coated), quartz, and smoky quartz.   42" X 55"   2010.

"Procession of the Three Worlds" depicts the three gunas as body, mind and spirit. The male and female archetypes are merging in cosmic harmony, illuminating that one and one is indeed three: object, observer, and the act of observation. (two lines make a third in the negative space between). The quartz inlaid in the star above their head radiates pure consciousness. The opalescent topaz inlaid in the calendar face above their hand shows consciousness refracting into the seven-fold, astral spectrum of thought. The smoky quartz on the figure's headdress represents that crystalline awareness incarnated into matter. The female form gestures toward the procession of time, as the male forms turns his gaze inward, in a balancing act of inner and outer universes.

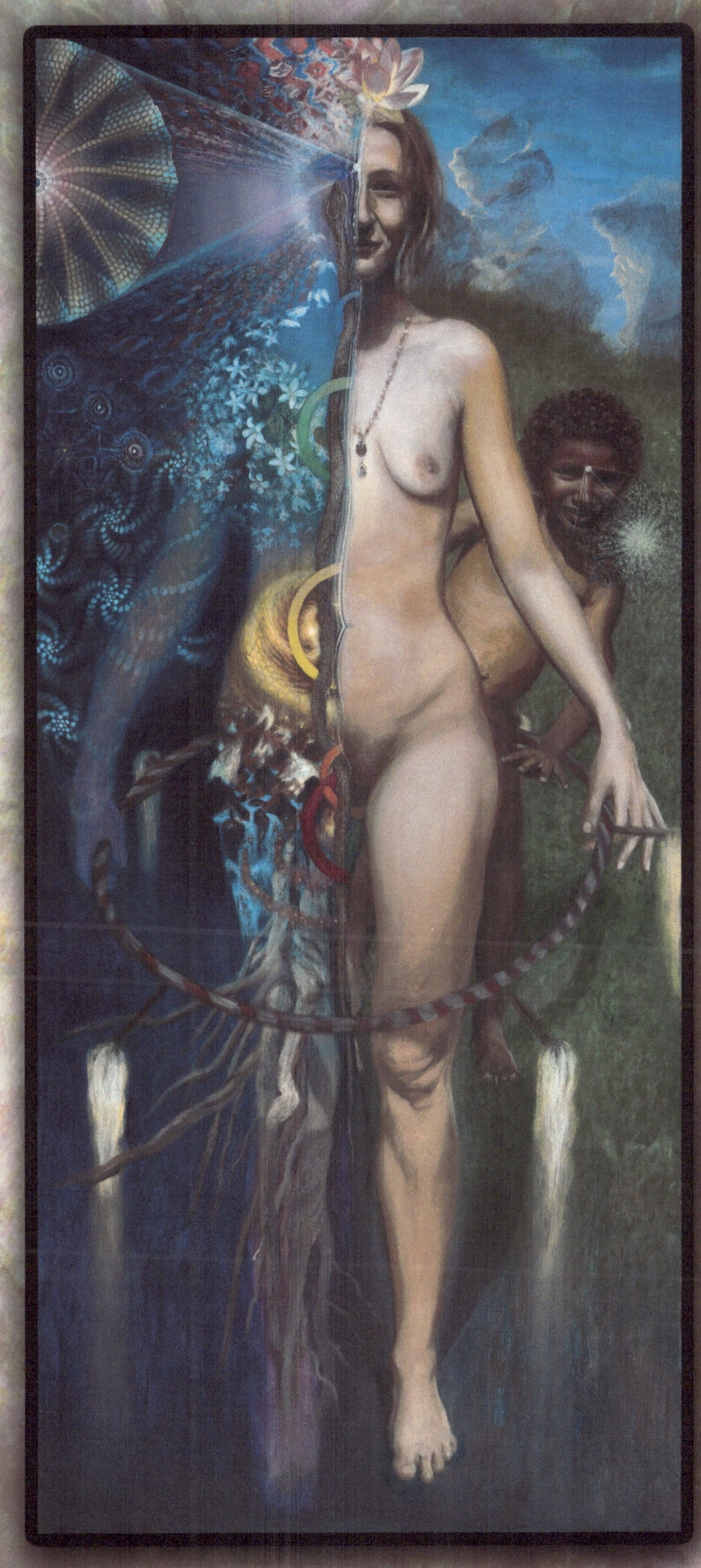

"Mother and Son, Passing the Torch of Vision"

Oil and acrylic on panel
80" X 36"   2008-2010

I am fascinated with the play of cycles revolving around an eternally still center.

The energy body surrounds the pure light-shaft, or shashumna running up the spine. The hula hoop revolves around the dancer. The eternal light within is passed through the cycle of generations.

The left half is the inner spiritual reality at the moment of Kundalini's awakening and ascent through the chakra system. The right half grounds the sacred vision into manifest matter, bringing it into daily life.

The entire kingdom of heaven can fit inside a single atom of our human body.

Love is the thread running through each molecular bead.

The flame of the torch of vision is passed from Brahman into Brahman.

"Durga Maya Lila"

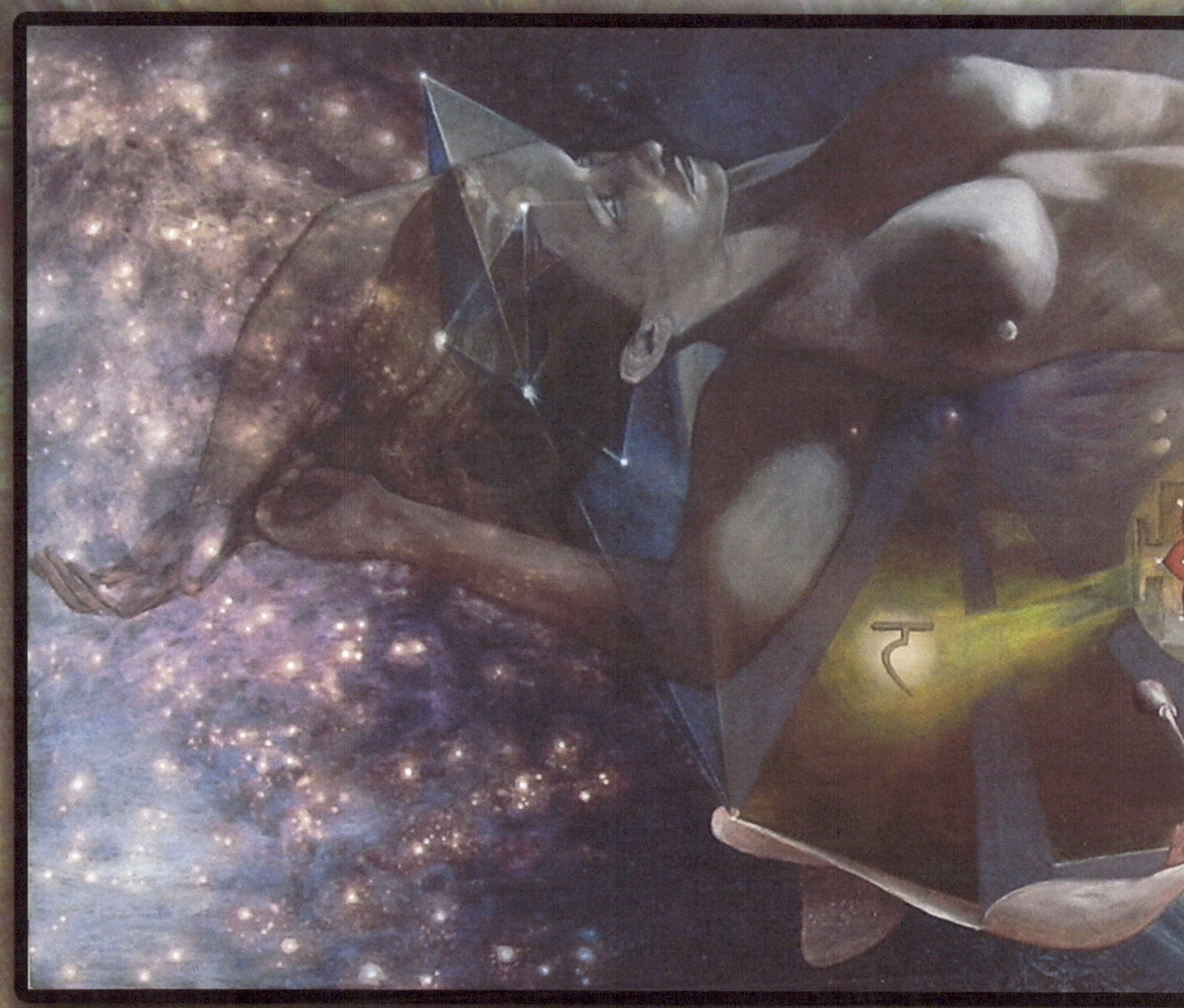

Durga is known as "she who is beyond reach". She is the absolute consciousness of divine reality. The central yantra is the hub of her presence, like silent
eye of a whirling hurricane. The yellow symbol emanating out to the left is the
seed mantra "Ra". Ra is the sound of manifestation; it is the fire which births
the cosmos. Maya is the illusory veil of creation, the fabric of space-time
covering the supreme truth of Durga. Lila is the divine play of the universe, the
process of creation spiraling around her sacred nucleus. The figure reclining
across the panel speaks of the soul's surrender to cosmic law, the play of the
Gods. She floats through the universe, allowing the changes to take place,
guiding her vessel across the ocean of transmigration.

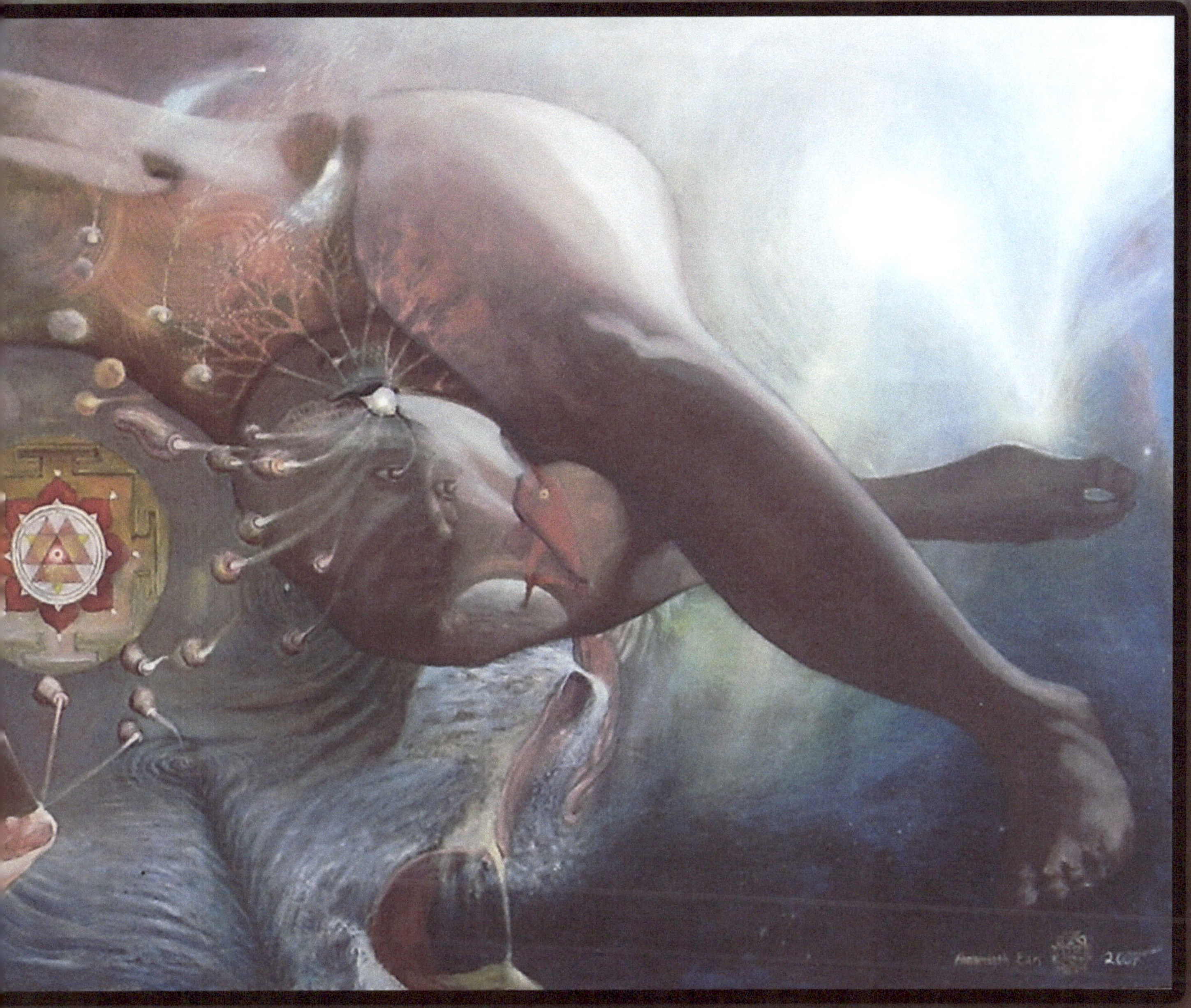

Acrylic on panel with inlaid lab-created ruby and natural quartz. 30" X 80". 2007-10

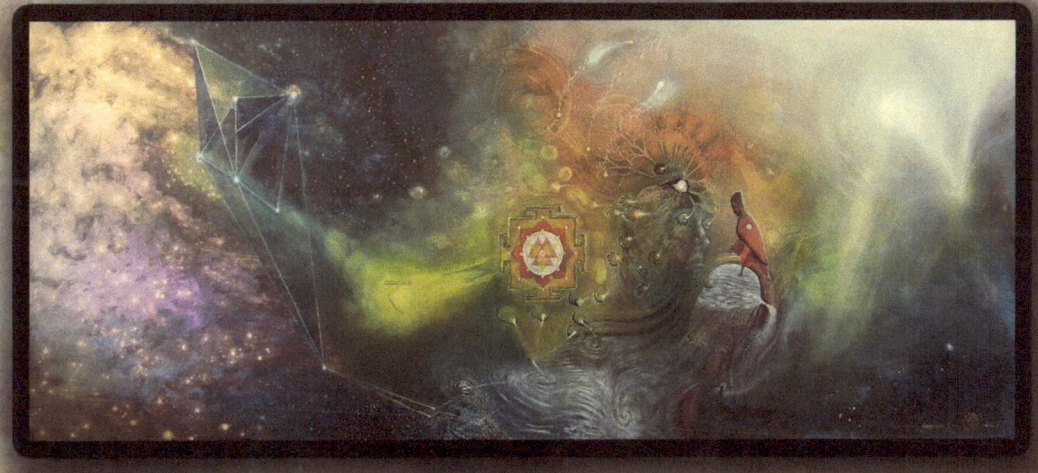

Previous version, before the main figure appeared.

"Three Worlds Triptych"

Acrylic and lab-created ruby cabochon on three boards with handmade wooden frames.

26" X 13"   2009

"The Divine Realm" depicts the mastery of consciousness and the subtle art of life's balance.

"The Middle Plane" depicts this world of fecundity, the creation of matter. The Shiva Lingam and Yoni base harmonize creation into Being. The Ruby center represents the sun's effulgence, allowing life to form. The animals and egg are symbols of life and growth.

"The Underworld" depicts the gateway to the afterlife's endlessly interconnected soul-matrix. An infant soul emerges, passing an elder who has completed his incarnation. This is the world of dreams, thought, and emotion. It governs all you call yourself that is not of flesh.

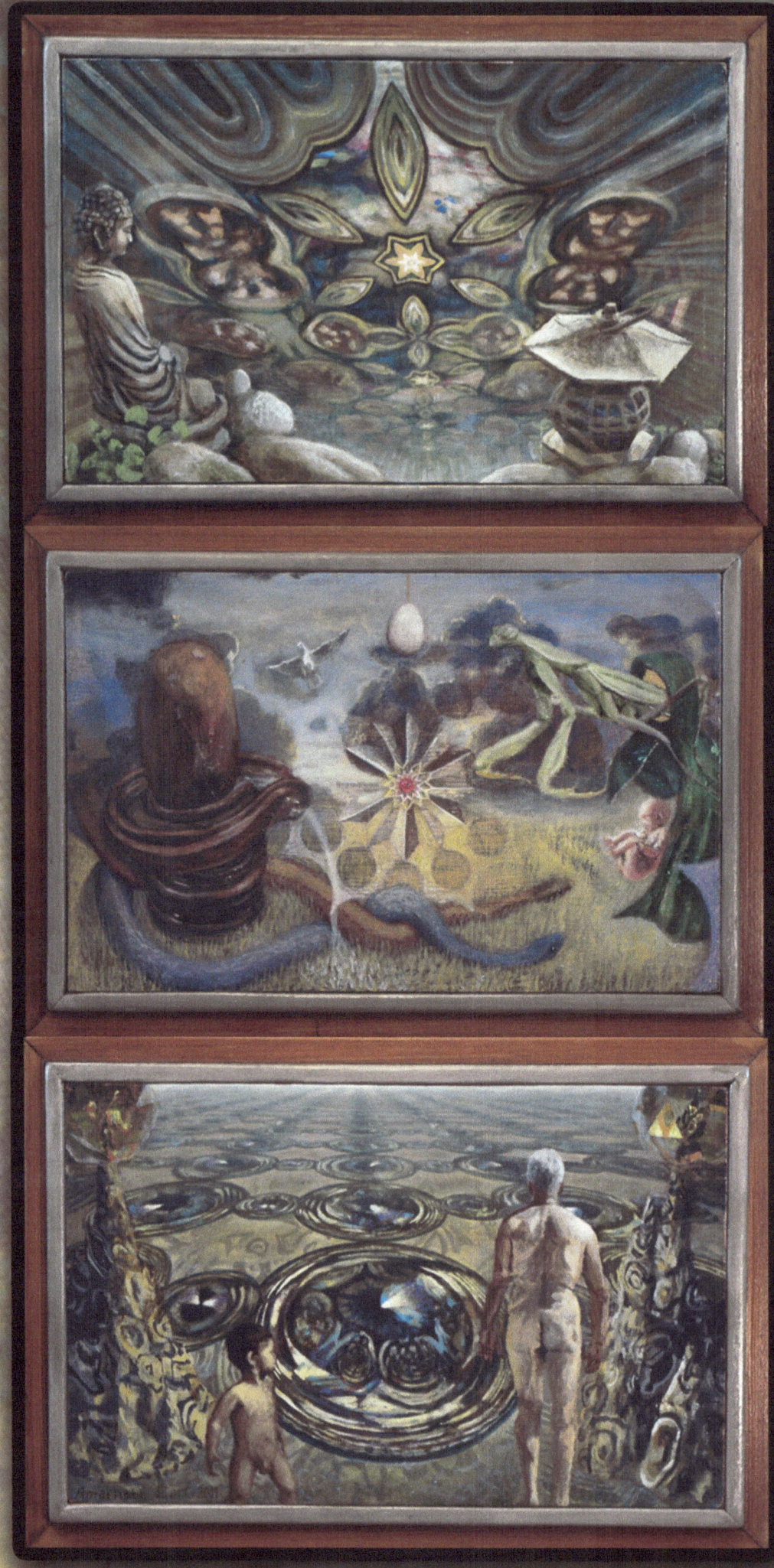

"Growth Rings"

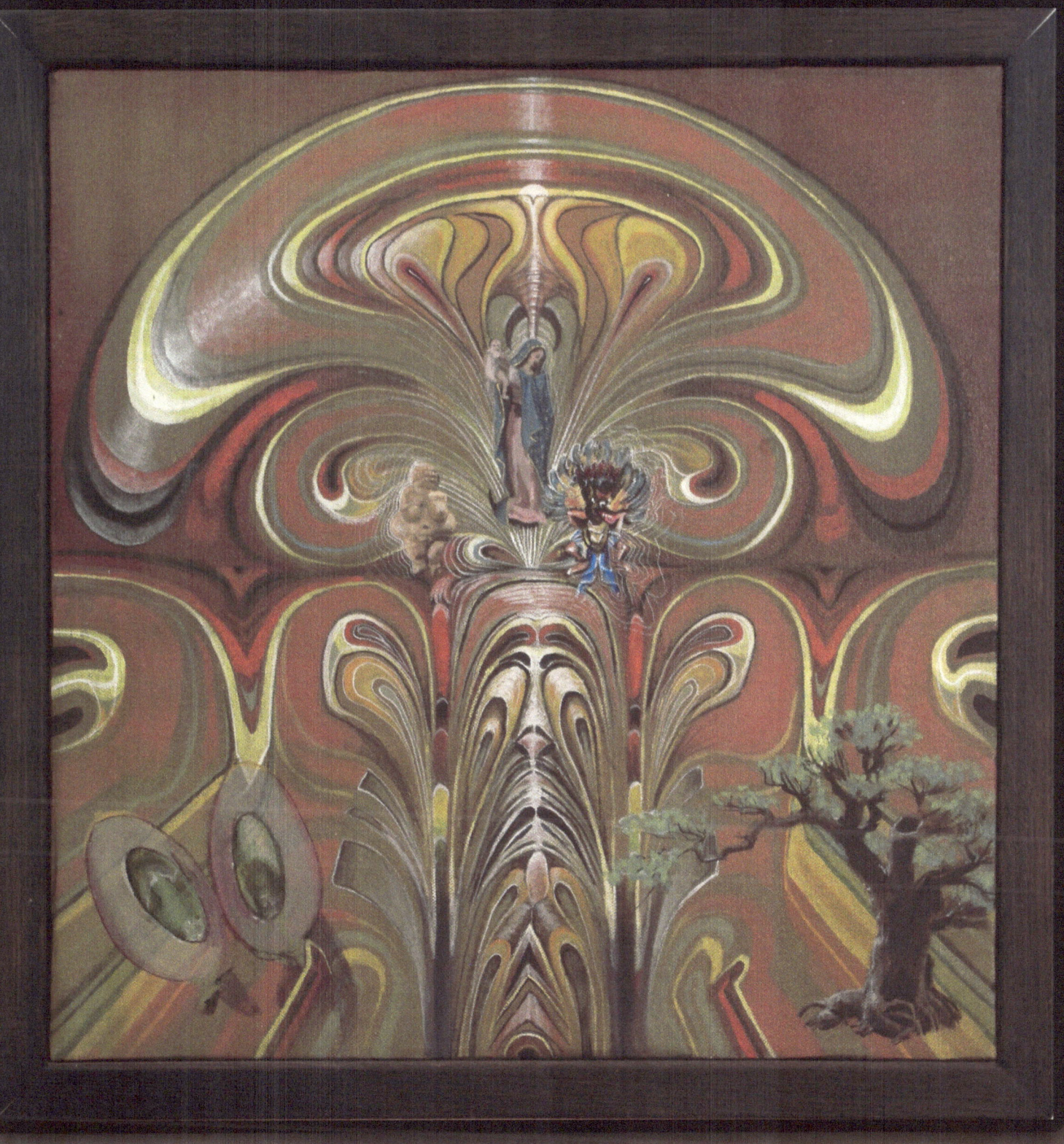

Acrylic on canvas.   18" X 18"   2007

Growth Rings is about cycles, especially the ultimate cycle: birth and death. The seed
and tree at the bottom show that both are creative forces, death being the flowering of
life. The Virgin Mary holds the Holy Child above the worldly cycles to His place in
divine reality {a changeless place}, while birth and death circle at her feet.

Spirit Orb Intro

Drift within
You are
light
vibrating.

Every
arising
thought
pulls you
ever closer
toward
your source.

Black hole
fingers run
along the
folds of
your brain,

smoothing
the intricate
mass into a
conical velvet
web-funnel

channeling
all of your
life-energy
toward
center.

God alone is
all there
was, is, or
ever will be.

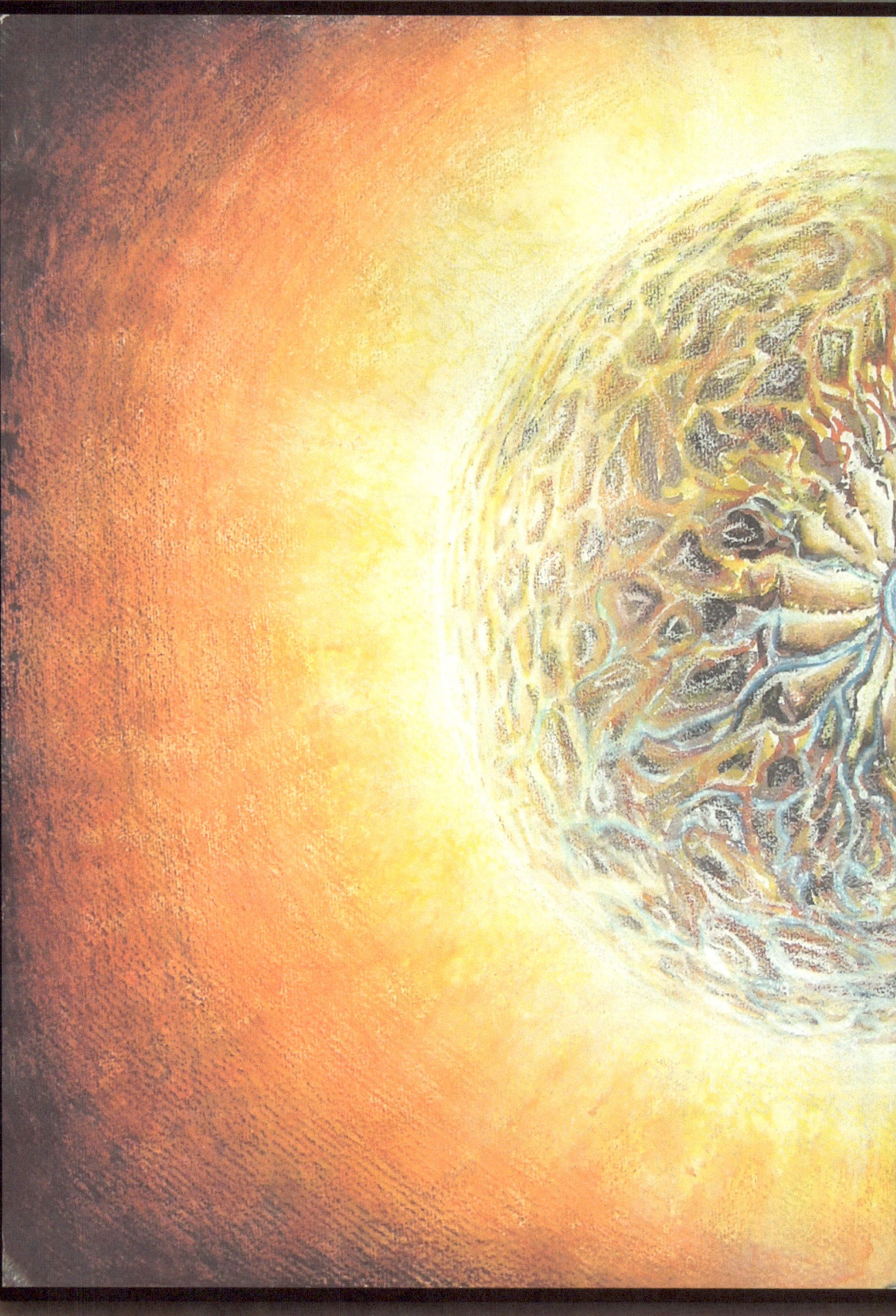

Watercolor, colored pencil, china marker in sketchbook

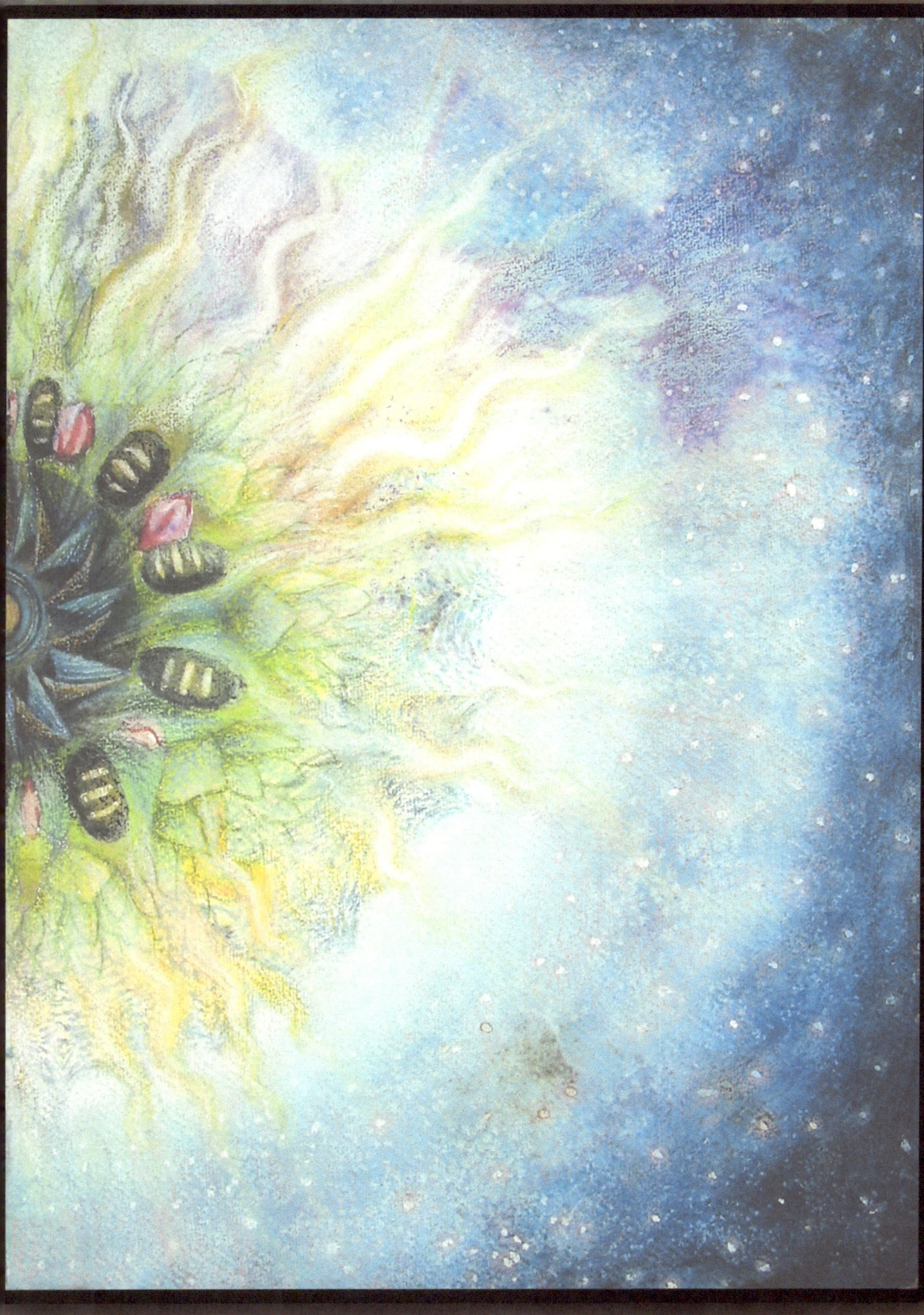

Spirit Orb Extro

Every action has an equal and opposite reaction

light vibrates so fast around the infinitely compresssed bindu of Shiva's black hole third eye that it inverts and explodes outward in a white hole effulgence.

Scatter all of your life-energy as stars across the universe,

like ashes into the sea.

God alone is all there was, is, or ever will be.

15" X 22"   2008

"Kundaleden"

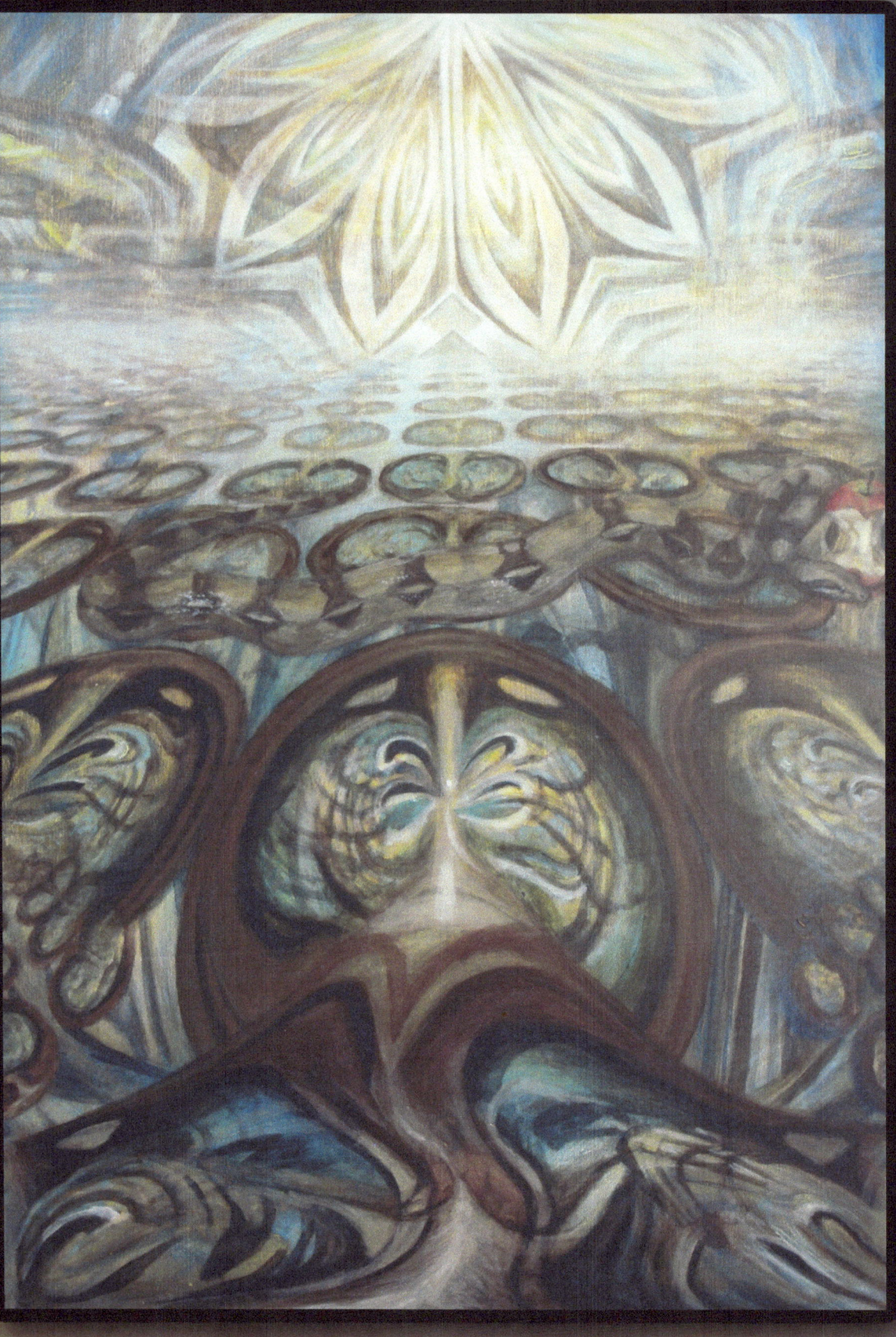

"Kundaleden" depicts two ways energy is expressed.

The dormant serpent follows sensory gratification in the infinite flatland of worldly existence, while the Kundalini serpent creates a vertical trajectory through all dimensions, rising to meet God.

Acrylic on cradled board.   34" X 24"   2009

"Vajra"

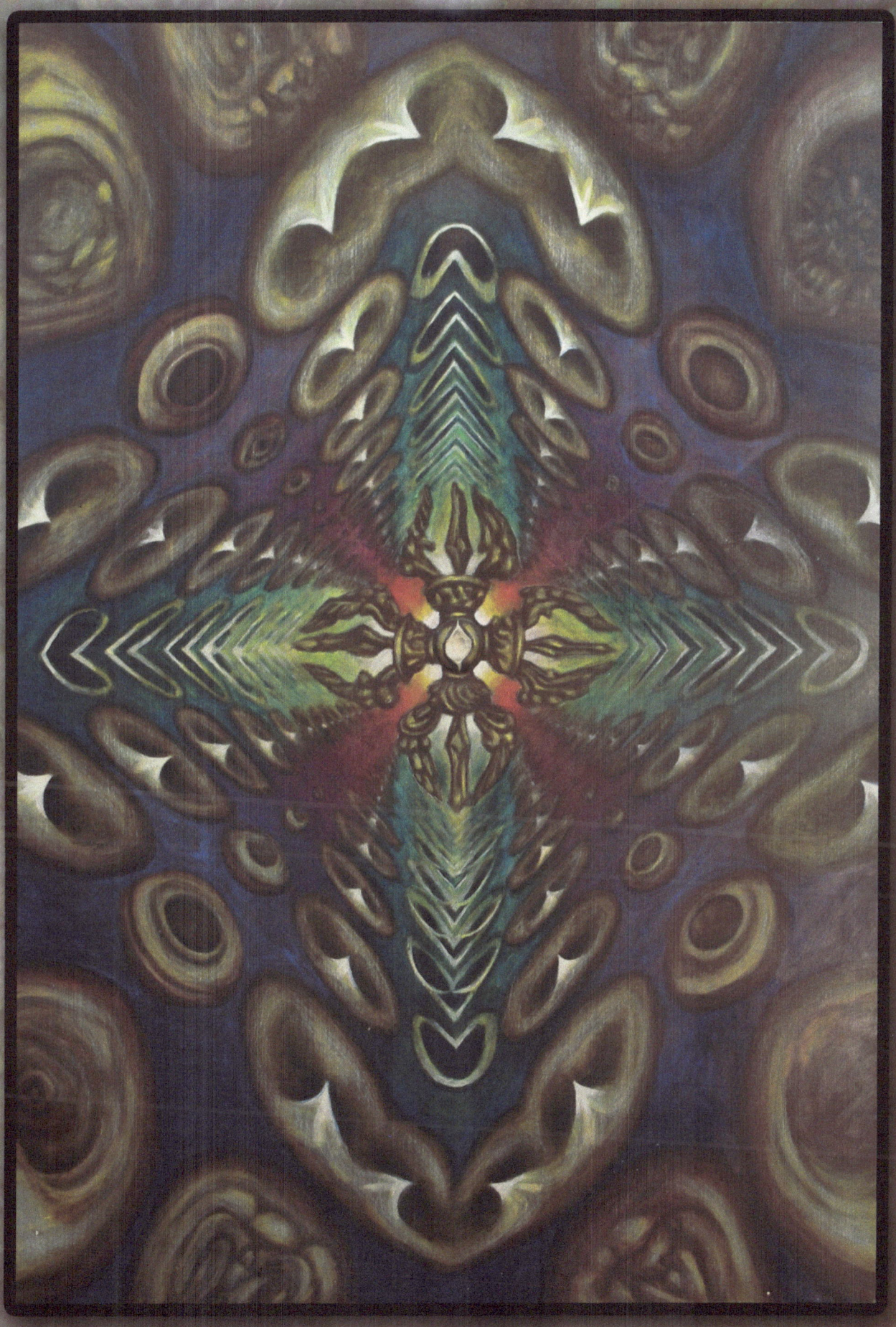

Acrylic on cradled board with Herkimer diamond.   34" X 24"   2009

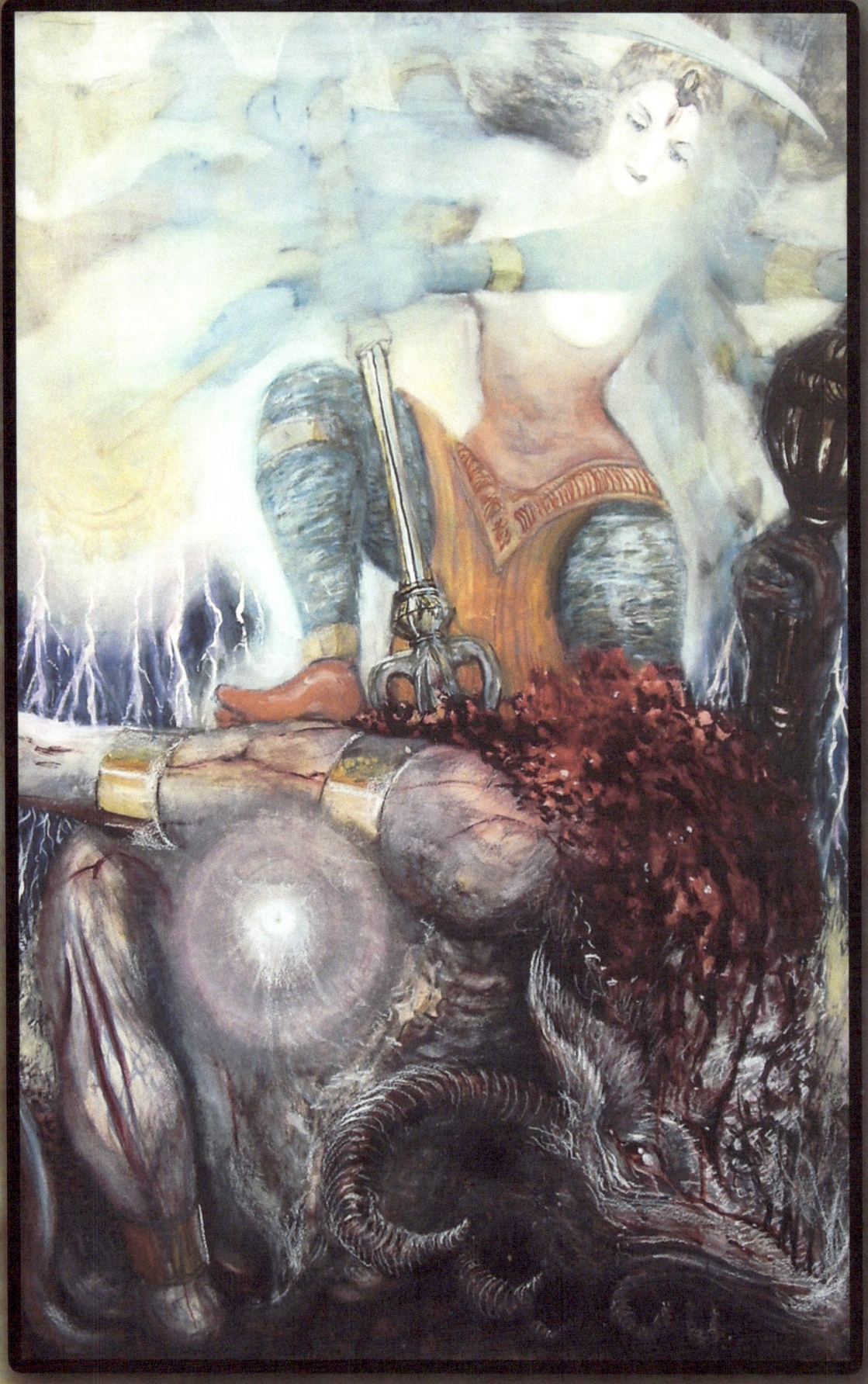

Durga is known as "She Who is Beyond Reach".

She is the unfathomable consciousness of divine reality.

This water-color depicts supreme truth defeating egoic ignorance.

Durga's fierce grace, lightninglike, transmutes the Buffalo Demon's form into the pure light of Being.

Watercolor on illustration board.   24" X 18".   2005

"Ardh-narishwara"

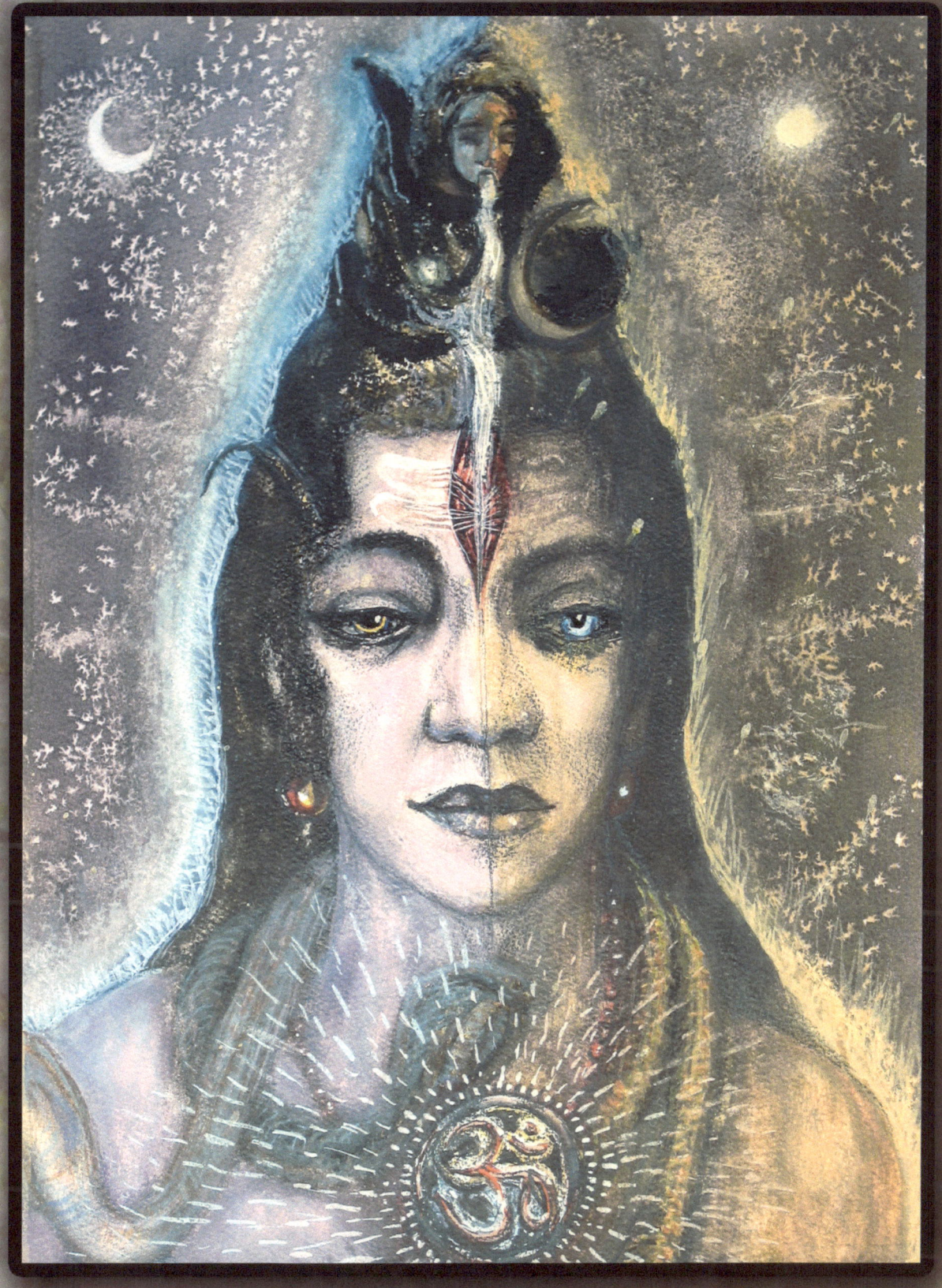

Watercolor on paper. 14" X 11". 2005

Ardh-narishwara is a hermaphroditic deity embodying a unified balance of
Shiva (divine masculine) and Shakti (divine femenine). AUM Namah Shivaya.

"Birth of Ganesh"

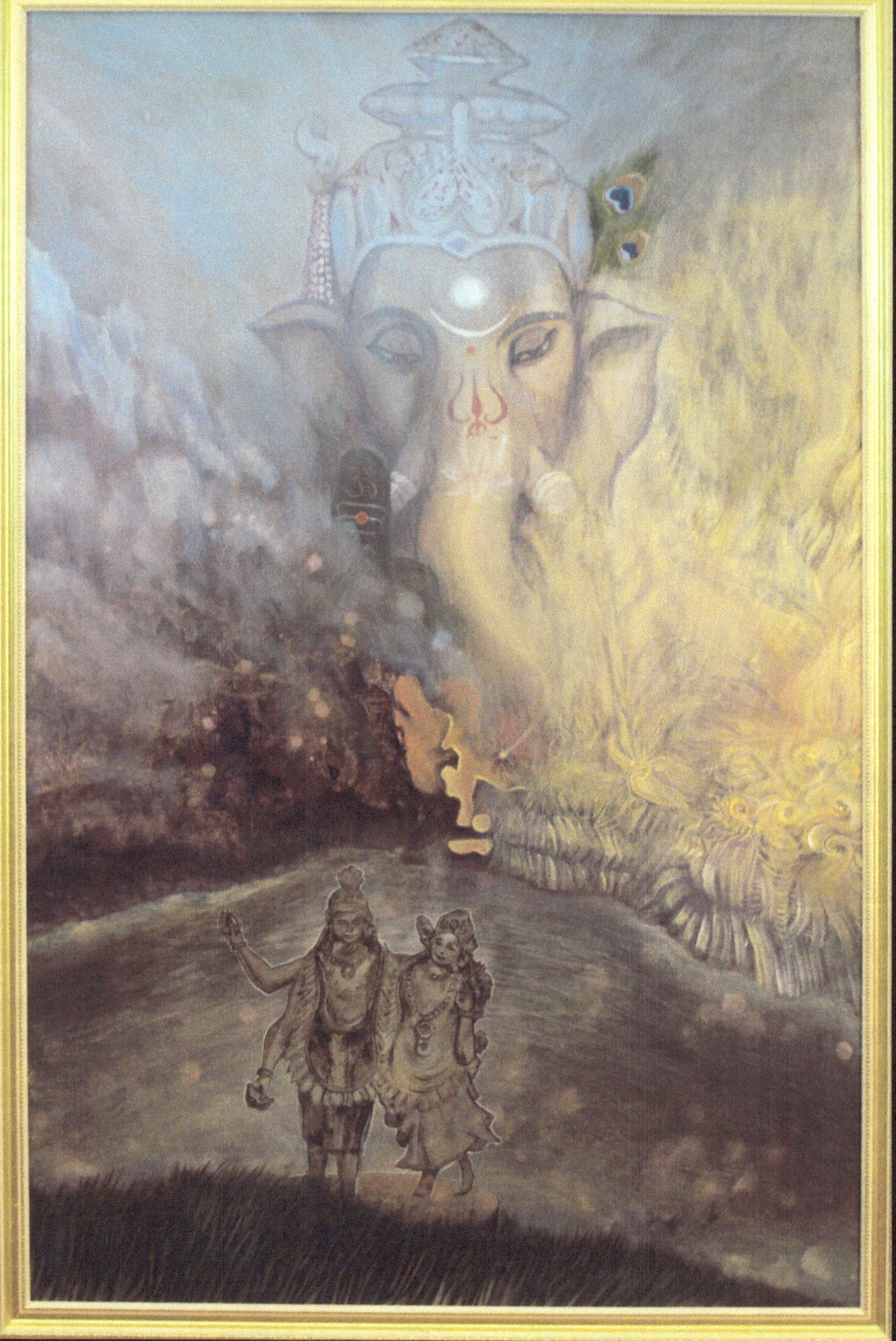

Shiva
and
Parvati

dancing

on
the
bank
of
eternity

create

through
their
divine
love

a
child
in
perfect
balance

Acrylic on canvas.　　36" X 24".　　2007

"Ganesh Murti"

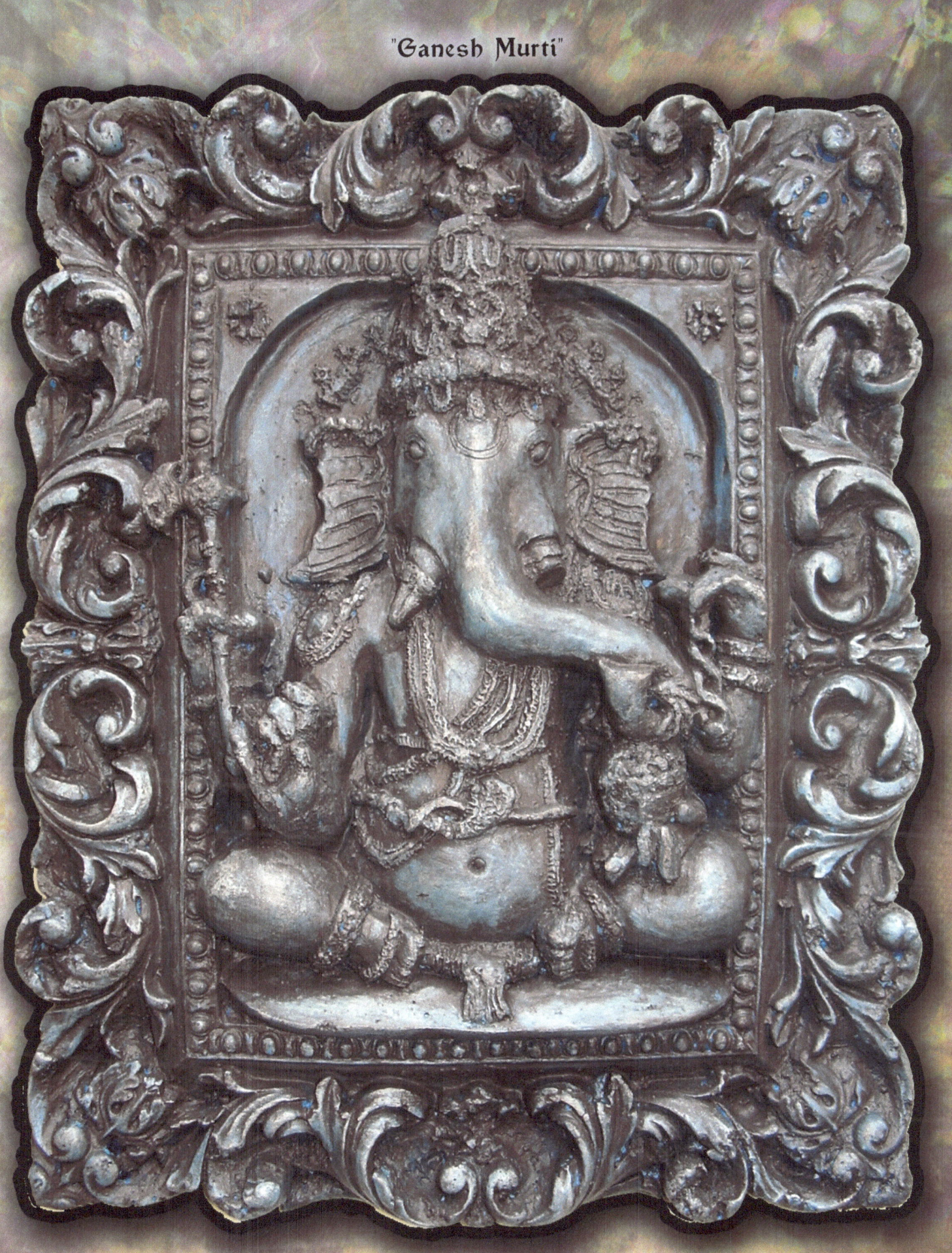

Varying edition of hand-painted plaster casts.   8" X 10".   2011

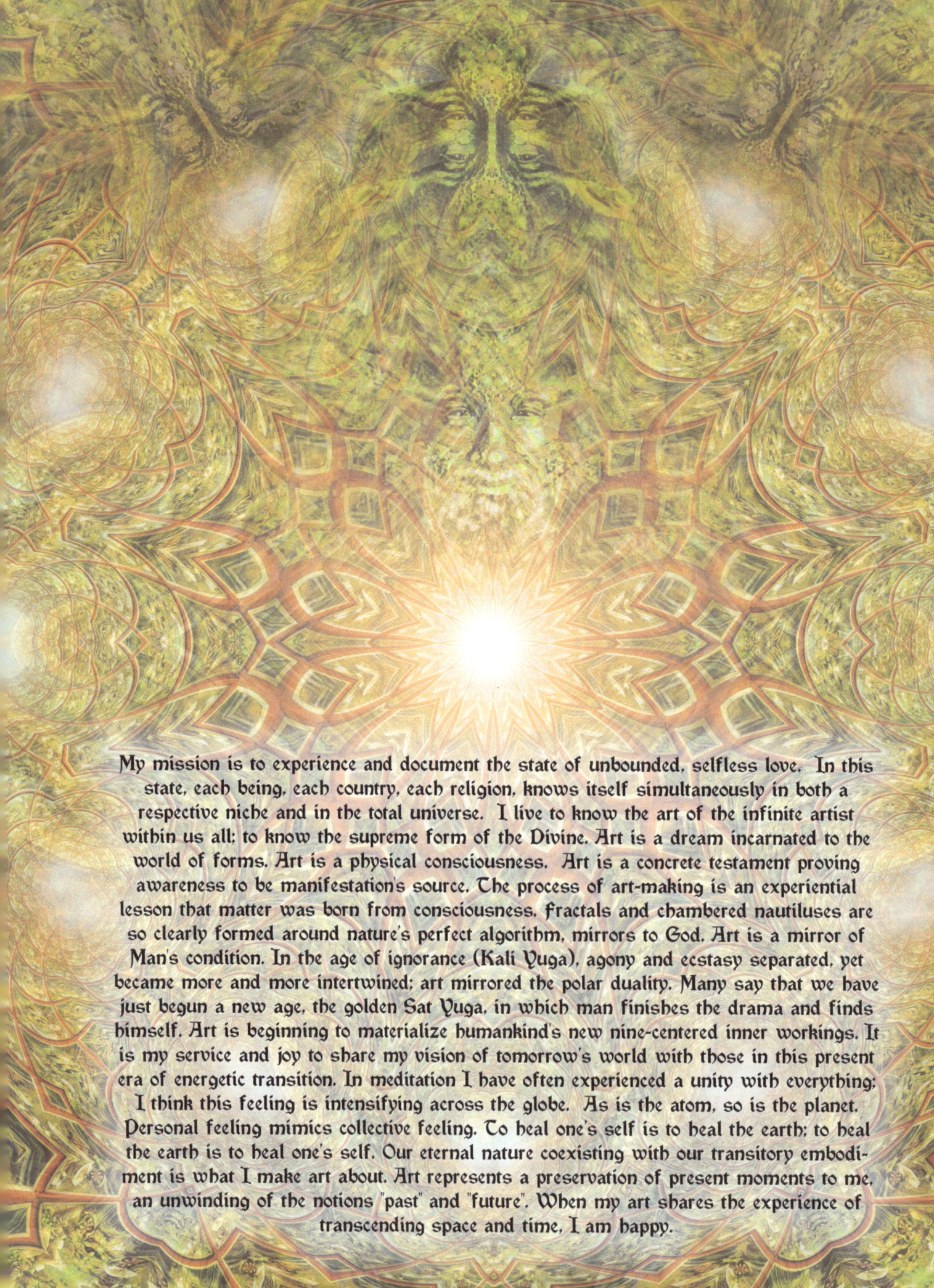

My mission is to experience and document the state of unbounded, selfless love. In this
state, each being, each country, each religion, knows itself simultaneously in both a
respective niche and in the total universe. I live to know the art of the infinite artist
within us all; to know the supreme form of the Divine. Art is a dream incarnated to the
world of forms. Art is a physical consciousness. Art is a concrete testament proving
awareness to be manifestation's source. The process of art-making is an experiential
lesson that matter was born from consciousness. Fractals and chambered nautiluses are
so clearly formed around nature's perfect algorithm, mirrors to God. Art is a mirror of
Man's condition. In the age of ignorance (Kali Yuga), agony and ecstasy separated, yet
became more and more intertwined; art mirrored the polar duality. Many say that we have
just begun a new age, the golden Sat Yuga, in which man finishes the drama and finds
himself. Art is beginning to materialize humankind's new nine-centered inner workings. It
is my service and joy to share my vision of tomorrow's world with those in this present
era of energetic transition. In meditation I have often experienced a unity with everything;
I think this feeling is intensifying across the globe. As is the atom, so is the planet.
Personal feeling mimics collective feeling. To heal one's self is to heal the earth; to heal
the earth is to heal one's self. Our eternal nature coexisting with our transitory embodi-
ment is what I make art about. Art represents a preservation of present moments to me,
an unwinding of the notions "past" and "future". When my art shares the experience of
transcending space and time, I am happy.

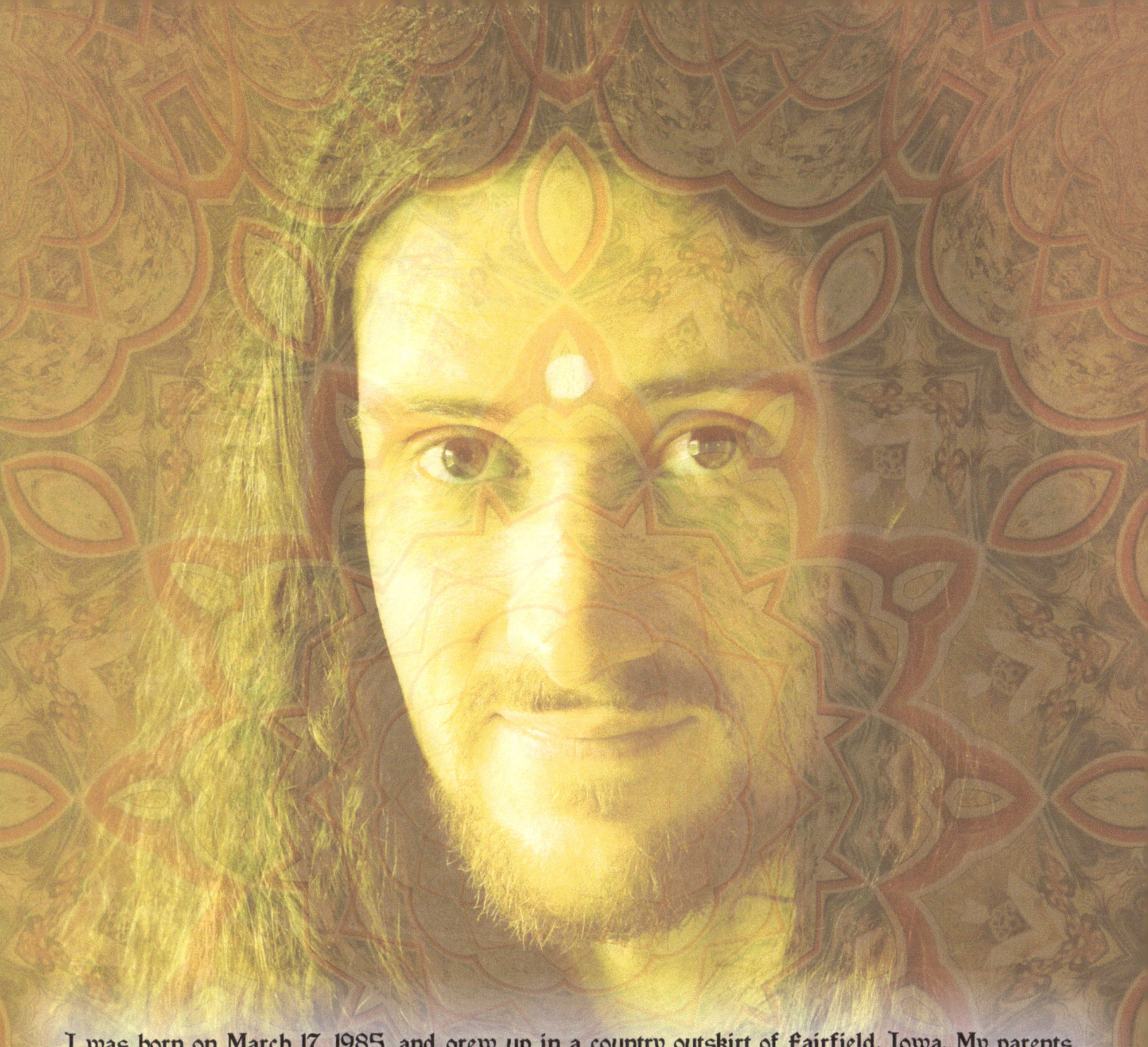

I was born on March 17, 1985, and grew up in a country outskirt of Fairfield, Iowa. My parents, Mark and Alexandra Stimson, had moved there to be involved with the blossoming Transcendental Meditation community and start a family. Much of my immediate and extended family members are artists and meditators; this lifestyle is in my lineage and upbringing. I was educated alongside my siblings, Albert and Rae, through Fairfield's community of home scholars. At fifteen, I left the familiarity of Fairfield to study visual art at Interlochen Arts Academy, a boarding arts high school in Michigan for two years. I returned to Fairfield before my senior year for self-study and re-centering. Next I journeyed to Baltimore, to attend Maryland Institute, College of Art. I ventured into an exploration of darkness and the unknown, fueled by the air of a hurting city. I made passionate works, observing with innocent awe that people carried so much pain on their backs and never found respite. I then decided the only way to study anything, especially art, is to study Self. I met Mata Amritanandamayi (Amma) in 2003 and she filled my life with love and meaning. In her divine presence, I saw my art and healing practices as not only a path to Self-Realization, but as a path of service to humankind. Amma brought me to the awareness that Lord Shiva is my beloved deity, and initiated me in his mantra. Amma gave me the name Amarnath, meaning "Lord Shiva, God beyond the Gods". I am currently meditating, painting, and practicing healing arts at OneDoorLand, in SE Portland, OR.

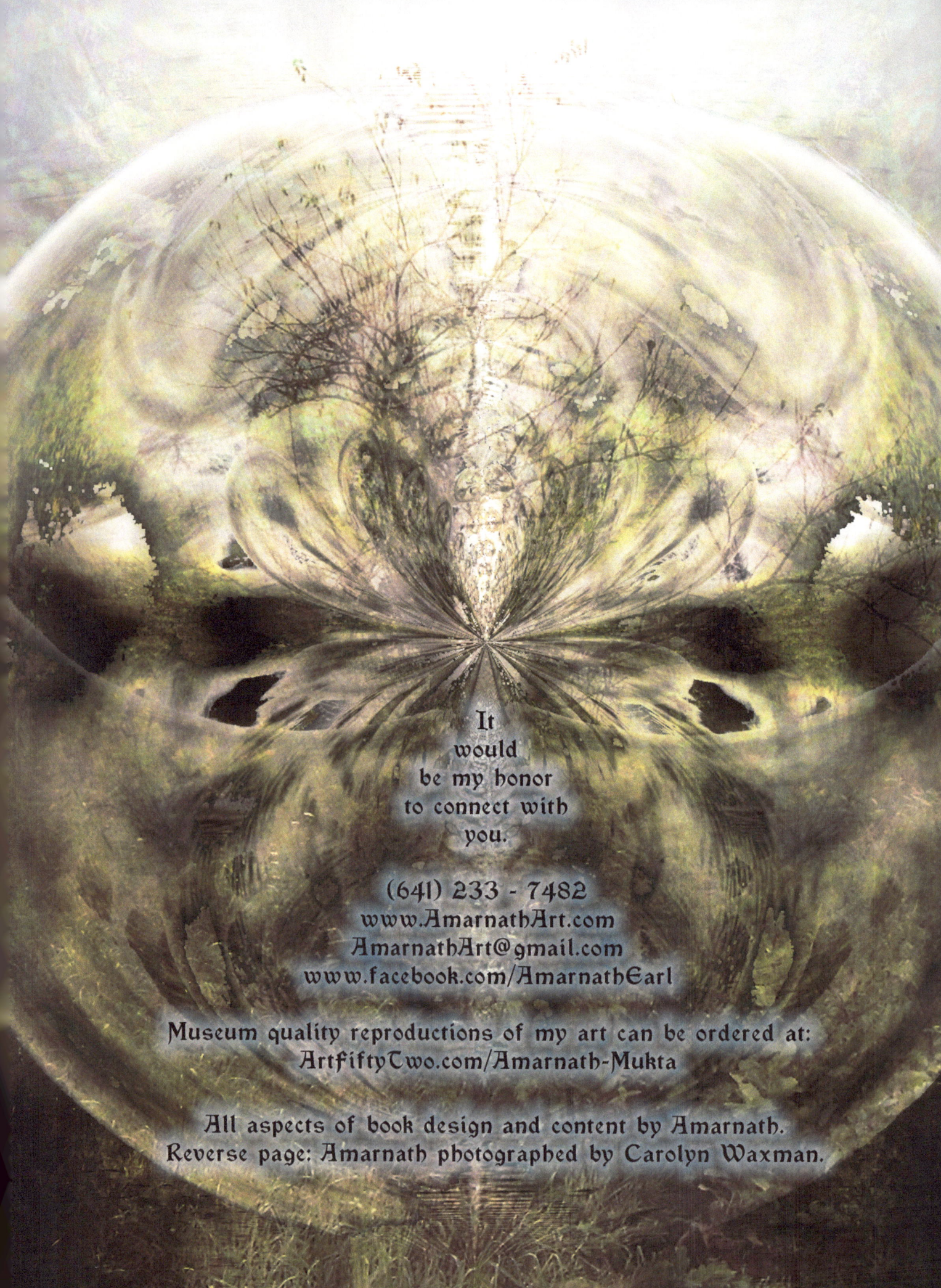

It
would
be my honor
to connect with
you.

(641) 233 - 7482
www.AmarnathArt.com
AmarnathArt@gmail.com
www.facebook.com/AmarnathEarl

Museum quality reproductions of my art can be ordered at:
ArtfiftyTwo.com/Amarnath-Mukta

All aspects of book design and content by Amarnath.
Reverse page: Amarnath photographed by Carolyn Waxman.

www.ingramcontent.com/pod-product-compliance
Lightning Source LLC
Chambersburg PA
CBHW050431180526
45159CB00005B/2494